WHO WRITES THE WAVES?

WHO WRITES THE WAVES?

Poems by Robin Amis

AGORA BOOKS

Hand bound by
TWO RIVERS PRESS, Aurora, Oregon, USA

Published by
Agora Books, China Hill, Brightling Road
Robertsbridge, East Sussex, England TN32 5EH
Tel: 0580 881137

in conjuction with
TWO RIVERS PRESS, Oregon 97002, USA

Also available in N. America from
PRAXIS INSTITUTE PRESS
275 High Road, Newbury, MA 01951
Tel: (508) 462 0563

Printed in Great Britain by
BPCC Wheatons Ltd., Exeter

© Robin Amis. No part of this book may be
reproduced in any form without permission
from the publisher, except for the quotation
of passages in criticism.

British Library Cataloguing-in-Publication Data:
A catalogue record for this book is
available from the British Library

Library of Congress catalogue card number:
92-80805

ISBN 1-872292-03-8

*To dear Lillian, who has learned so well
the language of the heart.*

CONTENTS

Introduction

I. THE IDENTITY KIT - A suite of poems
  O Secret Spring
  Common Land
  Stop Song
  The Mantle of Osiris
  When People Meet
  The Wells of Wisdom
  White Crane
  The Return of the Mysteries
  Softly the Song

II. THE DOOR INTO SUMMER
  I. Casey
  II. Milandrout
  III. And You
  IV. Merlin
  V. Strangers
  VI. Conjunction

III. POETRY OF PERCEPTION
  One Hand to the helm
  Pan comes dancing
  The eyes of love
  Vision
  All the Land

IV. PRAYERS
  Fragment
  Prayer No. 1
  Prayer No. 2
  Gethsemane Prayer
  Lent is a Time to Sing

Recollection
Dedication
Hymn to Iacchus
Pardes Rimonnim
The Love of Woman

V. SOME SHORT POEMS
Two-edged sword
Work
May Song
But one solution
Ember sings to the Tall Trees
O Most Kind Comfort
Helen of the Thousand Faces
Work
Icarus

VI. BROTHER CAIN

VII. EARLY POEMS
Who Calls
Burrow Bridge
Jirian
The Great Experiment
Had I such Heart
When you are there
Incantation
The Fear of Freedom
Remember My Love
The Fountain of Lies
Could it be you?
The other Eden of the mind
The Phoenix Flies
Where is the Door of Summer?
Every Instant has its Meaning
The White Horse Rides
To Bind Bright Freedom
Did the Green Star?

Introduction

When one first comes to know somebody in the maturity of their life there is often a sense of incompleteness as if one were starting to read a book many chapters from the beginning. The Robin Amis that I have known for the past several years as a philosopher, teacher and writer on Eastern Orthodox theology had always seemed to have a somewhat enigmatic side to his nature. It was only when I recently had the chance to read this collection of poems that he wrote as a young man twenty or thirty years ago that his personality came into full focus for me. My reading of the poems was enriched by my experience of his later writings and, in its turn, his current work on Christian esotericism was illuminated by the ardour and musicality of the poetry.

Seen in the symmetry of these two phases, Amis's life assumes the character of a spiritual adventure with all the danger and excitement that that implies. I am reminded of the French poet René Daumal, who died in 1944 at the age of thirty-six, a geographer of such spiritual journeys, whose writing can help to establish the polarities of Amis's work in a single perspective. For a number of writers and artists in France the years of the Occupation were a time for introspection and truth-telling, and the output from that dark period possesses a singular clarity and insight. Daumal's extraordinary unfinished novel Mount Analogue was one of the masterpieces of the time telling the story of an expedition in search of a mysterious mountain. It was a mountain normally rendered invisible by an eccentric curvature of time and space but known to the philosopher-teacher, who led the little party of uneasy souls on their quest, to be visible and accessible at certain instants to certain people. When this threshold had been passed the ascent of Mount Analogue could begin, with all its perils and victories. As I have followed Amis's work over recent years I have been repeatedly recalled to Daumal's strange expedition in search of the invisible. Even my first meeting with Amis was more metaphor than social encounter. I was spending a night as a guest at the Greek Orthodox monastery of Simonaspetra on Mount Athos. As I was being welcomed by the monks I saw, through a doorway that led on to a high balcony, the unlikely figure of a man dressed as if for an evening walk in the Gloucestershire countryside. He was gazing through the haze of the setting sun towards the great triangular profile of Mount Athos itself. Although an Englishman out of context I sensed an odd inevitability about his presence there. I was intrigued to know what had brought him to such a place and why he seemed to be strangely at ease there so at home on the Holy Mountain. Now that I have read his poems the answer is clearer than it has ever been.

His poems are full of questions. Of course, it is in the nature of young poets to ask questions but, whereas most leave those questions hanging gracefully in the air, Amis chose to set his poetry aside and to embark on the hard road of seeking real answers. Such an undertaking involves 'courage locked into a profound integrity of purpose' as a commentator on Daumal once put it. The poetic sensibility must be borne into the drier climate of the intellect. A desert crossed, the dryness endured, disappointments faced, yet through it all the need to keep the precious burden of the poet's questions intact. Daumal's spiritual geography is not for the faint-hearted. Yet, as in the search for Mount Analogue, a certain moment may come to those who have lasted the journey when a door opens and the almost forgotten questions find their answers. Perhaps this is the 'door to summer firm beneath winter snow' that Amis speaks of in one of his best poems. The door that connects the chamber of the mind with the chamber of the heart, the door leading to wholeness and reconciliation.

Knowing Amis's recent writing on Eastern Orthodox spirituality I can, with hindsight, see innumerable links with his early poems, deepening my understanding of them. Indeed, to Amis himself it must seem even more remarkable to see his mature destination so clearly marked in his beginnings.

This does not mean that the poems cannot be appreciated for themselves alone. They stand as an impressive self-sustained body of work. Amis's poetic voice is individual and authentic and the verses possess both the gravity and beauty to bear many re-readings.

In one of his rare poems written recently — an affectionate tribute to his friends the monks of Athos — Amis reveals that, on his many journeys to the Holy Mountain, the muse that he addressed so boldly as a young poet has, after all, been his companion there. He is a lucky man.

Donald Hamilton Fraser, R.A.

I

THE IDENTITY KIT

A suite of poems

O SECRET SPRING

O joy, such joy, that I should know
This hidden spring to overflow,
As He Who causes things to move
Refills the secret wells of love.
O rich, how rich the burning tree
That flames eternally for me.
O bright, so bright the secret eye
That sudden makes the blind man see.
But greater miracle than these
The birds, the earth, the autumn trees:
In cell, in atom, meson, quark
A brilliance stirring deep in dark —
One light for each, one light for all
Intense for great, exact for small.
And hidden, hidden in the dark
The builder, keeper, blessed spark.

O joy, such joy that you should know
This hidden spring to overflow.

London, 1972

COMMON LAND

A freeform sonnet

Had I no eye nor sense to shape the dream,
Nor ear to bind with blindness the dark mind,
Then would I write brief treatise to my theme
Whose meaning now is written on the wind
With words of moving meaning, softly signed.
For we've all doorways to the common land,
Panes that refract, and so distract the mind
Bridges by which the ocean deeps be spanned,
Sweet bonds to gyve, that he who sleeps is blind.
While liberty dies wasting of neglect,
By rule of freedom bound, in its defect,
Mind guides blind mind through pathways indirect.
    Yet while each eye a different dream espies,
    Truth knows one single I for all these eyes.

London, 1972

STOP SONG

Suffer the dancing feet to laugh,
Then turn on sorrow as a bear at bay,
For rare's the pain that is not self-made grief
That dies beneath the brighter light of day -
Yet such uncommon pain is fire enough
To blood the untried blade of the young heart,
All sad flames else of folly, or of art.

Now hold
The runing fingers of the exorcist.
Swift drive the shaman to his grave.
Now stop,
To see with child's eye a world
Where death, and change, and shock of birth
Alone can tempt the tempered heart
To flee the constancy of Earth.

See in all flesh upon its round
That old dead dragon writes his way anew,
Though thrice-born men forgive the worm his wound
In glory at the wonder day can show.
So snowflake life again with thorns is crowned
For those who see, within each shrouded soul
The shadowed sun of spirit, still and whole.

Now dream
To see the sun that outshines pain:
Eat of that midday manna then.
So stop
To find within the heart the place
Of that lone self
That smiles behind each face.

Bristol, 1963

THE MANTLE OF OSIRIS

What wine is this
Distilled upon human earth
Brings some new light of sense to silent birth?
What hand, by overshadowing
Makes sleep, despair and dreaming take to wing?
What choral voice
Beyond the reach of words
Shall shape itself to silence and so sing?

Who to all men
The triple light
Of strength, of love, of vision
Now will bring?

Who bears the mantle of the King?

London, 1970

WHEN PEOPLE MEET

Who writes these symphonies of passing men,
That meetings come together into streams
And streams to rivers, rivers to ocean flow
Time, and time again? For what is time
That can so stop and link these island minds
Into an unguessed future?
What strange winds
Through many-peopled sleeping Leviathan
Of mismatched dreams,
Blow towards man
As man will one day be?
Who writes the waves upon the sea?

Paris, 1970

WHITE CRANE

A memory to marsh-people, a symbol to the Masters of the Far East, a feeling that finds its place in the sky of our hearts.

White crane flying,
Far from his tall-cloud strand;
White crane flying,
The flat wings that walk on the wind.

White crane calling,
Empty the ocean's reply:
White crane sailing,
Shadow that crosses the sky.

White crane waiting,
Where the sea and the sand become one,
White crane watching,
For the turtle that sings in the sun.

White crane sleeping,
By the black river at rest,
White crane peaceful,
The waiting is over at last.

THE RETURN OF THE MYSTERIES

Knock. Knock. Knock.
An old face walks the cold streets on a dark night,
knocking on the marked doors and calling,
Calling to the God within,
Calling to wake the dead.
And see, at Christmas flowers the thorn
In Avalon midwinter thorn
And midnight waking.

Knock. Knock. Knock.
Serpent staff on marble floor,
Knocking on the stone hearts, and calling,
Calling to the god within,
Calling to wake the dead.
And hear, midsummer on the mound
By Dion's tower on witching ground
Dreams are a-leaping.
Lie you sleeping?

The pomegranate seed is ripe.
A dream needs tending, guarding, watering.
I have seen a strange glow
In a mans eyes,
And watched a man happy
In a bus queue in Holborn,
And the street lamps are going out
One by one, all over England.

And see where twines the mistletoe,
Sign of the brothers of the bough
And bright heart breaking.

                              Knock. Knock. Knock.
Dionysus awake.
One man from a thousand take.
And from a thousand such one more
To lead them to the other shore.
Dionysus awake,
And melt the heart as it doth break,
For wax that melts
New shape shall take
And new life live with loving.

New music in the silence stands,
That sounds alone to reborn hands.
I have seen the warmth of a voice
Tease away wrinkles from an old face
And a warehouse off Old Street
Filled with an uncreated light,
And ordinary men happy
To stand an hour, still, in silence.
And in an old house in Stepney
A young man laughed as he died
And planted seeds of hope
In three tired hearts.
                              Knock. Knock. Knock.

                       London, 1970

SOFTLY THE SONG

(Dedicated to the 2000 or so monks of Mount Athos, who would rather hear a man sing for love of God, than listen because of his skill.)

Softly the song of love is sung
That sudden lights the day of man.
Listen, listen,
Catch it who catch it can, the song
That steals the silence.

Lowly the lay of love is learned
That soothes the pain of doubting man.
Listen, listen,
Catch it who catch it can, the lay
That leads the sundered soul to pray.

Slowly the day delights the apse
As dawn descends the frescoed wall,
Listen, listen,
Catch it who catch it can, the ray
That turns the inner night to so bright day.

Gloucestershire, 1988

II

THE DOOR INTO SUMMER

A dream mythology of 20th Century man.

The Door into Summer

I. CASEY

There are those who frequent the glitter of markets
Seeking the Summer in the bargain world,
Or in the shape of carved wood,
Of beaten brass, seeking.
For such, summer is hard to find, though Spring
Leaps sometimes in response to profit,
While winter follows close upon
The smallest loss.
Casey is one of those.

There are those who seek renewal in the country
Looking at tree and hill to throw to them
Some hint of hidden sunshine,
Some future freedom, looking.
For such, summer is hard to find, 'though peace
May draw them homeward when they're unaware
And only searching blinds them,
Binds them to winter.
Casey is one of those.

> For who has found Summer out of season,
> Power beyond the hour,
> Joy beyond all reason?
> Who has known
> The peace beyond possession
> Who has followed the sun's profession?

The Door into Summer

II MILANDROUT

There are those who walk their own way to darkness,
Seeking a god thought-formed in fickleness:
As though stone owns mountain;
Though stone and steppe are one in substance.
So schemes Milandrout.

There are those who turn
The bright prayer-wheel of thought
Around the axis of their own self-doubt.
So spinning
Weave their way wandering to sorrow
Half borne. The fire that warms no hearth.
When fancy's fires are banked
They are seen sleeping.
So dreams Milandrout.

    For who has found
    The open door of prison:
    The lone door, his own door,
    Different for each person.
    Who has surfed
    To the crest of cruel compassion,
    Ridden on the wave
    And opened to the sea of love?

The Door into Summer

III - AND YOU?

What to you are the dead tomes, the dry bones
Of other men's dreams?
What the unfilled promise
Of simple summer to the heart seeking warmth
In status and the susurration of crowds?
My door is not your door,
Your door is not mine:
What then are words worth against
The touch of affection's hand, the flush
Of anger as the heart flees death in fury?
What use is the door to childhood
Buried under the years, the old tears,
The child's fall
From play To purpose?

> *For who has found*
> *The winter gate to Summer?*
> *Hidden door, forbidden door,*
> *The great bronze gate*
> *Of peace.*
> *Who has found*
> *The joy beyond delusion?*
> *Who has reached desire's conclusion?*

The Door into Summer

IV MERLIN

Some there are who enter as conqueror upon the paths
Of the old dragon of the world. Singing
Songs of summer beauty. Shaping
The hardened roads of recklessness. Binding
With adamant bonds of manhood
The myriad demons of the inward pit. Constraining
The pulsing forces of their natural wit
That from the very earth springs a bright flame,
Burning to fusion.
Merlin is one of those.

Some there are who weave a web of Spring to spell
Approaching Summer.
Some to whom birds sing
A simple song of truth: whose laughter leaps to love:
Who walking lone through winter, turn and stand
Confirmed in fellowship at need,
And when the doorway is at hand
They enter gladly.
Merlin is one of those.

For who has grasped
The peace beyond all passion?
Who allowed the sun's bright light to fashion
All his flesh? Who now
Reaps what he did not sow?

The Door into Summer

V. STRANGERS

*Some who are strangers yet to those they love,
And friends to strangers, following some trace
By sunlight laid in their most mortal flesh,
Come sudden on their door and sudden enter.
So sudden is their story simply told.
For what means alchemy to him
Who has sufficient gold?*

VI. CONJUNCTIO

*Silence is all true love. Speech knocks
Often with empty hands upon the heart's door
Yet moves the light heart softly to its home,
Opens the mind to sunshine, and awakes
From our cold firestone flame that so will clothe
The mortal soul that it may stand in love.*

London, 1970

III

THE POETRY OF PERCEPTION

ONE HAND TO THE HELM

Now that the walk is almost over
Here is the trust I will keep for thee;
One hand to the helm,
One foot to the path,
One heart to the grave
To set you free.
Pray to the Lord
When you are lonely
That what this means
You soon shall see.

Now that the dream-time heralds waking
Here is the watch I have kept for thee;
One hand to the helm,
One foot to the path,
One heart that died
To set you free.
Pray to the Lord
When you are lonely,
That what this means
You too shall see.

Bristol, 1964

PAN COMES DANCING

Once upon a while when the clouds blow long
Pan comes dancing with his secret song.
Pan comes dancing, chancing, glancing
Turning to your yearning
With a step that you aspire to,
Leaping to your weeping
With a bright fuelled fire.

Once upon awhile when the trees leap budding
Pan pipes the pitch of the melody of Spring,
Pan comes playing, praying, swaying,
Turning to your yearning
With a step that you aspire to.
Leaping to your weeping
With a bright fuelled fire.

Pan comes singing such a song of light,
Pan comes singing, swinging, ringing
Turning to your yearning
With a step that you aspire to.
Leaping to your weeping
With a bright fueled fire.

Bristol, 1964

THE EYES OF LOVE

*A stranger's greeting
Passing in the street.
A dream suspended
and a sleep of thought
Complete forgetting of the buyer and the bought.
A glance entrancing brings me to myself,
and what was empty
suddenly is wealth.
The newest thing
is suddenly the old:*
    *The eyes of love
      Perceive a different world.*

*A shard of sunlight
Fractured on the path,
A glimpse of weakness
Strengthening a life,
A foolish question that lets in the light,
slays self-assertion and excises doubt.
The whirling word
Is instantly made still,
And what was empty wond'rously is full;
The wings of envy suddenly are furled.*
    *The eyes of love
      Perceive a different world.*

London, 1969

VISION

Sudden the sparrows fly, sensing the eagle,
Still stands the plover as the wide wings pass.
Swift is peace split upon the blade of lightning.
Wide the wind lays its rows upon the grass
And sharp contraction breaks the strongest glass.

ALL THE LAND

Upon the thought, the sight, the voice of you
Flies up my love upon the swan's strong wing.
Now with your touch each vessel in the flesh does sing
Such Summer leaping laughter that my dreams
Are all o'ercome. Your beauty then does stand
Symbol of all the beauty in the land
And all the land stands true.

London, 1969

IV

PRAYERS

FRAGMENT

You ask me now of all my life
More strength than I have known,
That all my sorrow should be hid,
And all my joy be shown.

PRAYER No. 1

Open the gate.
Empty I wait.
Let me come in
To the warm.
Give me to eat, bread of my life,
Bear me up calmly.
Where there's no harm.

Open, my heart.
(How quietly Thou knockest!)
My eyes are thine.
Alone I am blind.
Here on Your altar
In dedication
My hands,
And my heart,
And my mind.

PRAYER No. 2

Turning heart inward
Wait on the Lord,
Then as the silence flows,
Gently letting it fall,
The seed word. The name.

With head preserve it.
With heart cherish it.
With inner speech say it.
The seed word. The name.

Into the silent mind
Still as clear water
Pure as fine platinum
Gently letting it fall,
The seed word. The name.

With head preserve it.
With heart cherish it.
With inner speech say it.
The seed word. The name.

Just for the sake of it,
Demanding naught of it,
In its own time
Gently letting it fall,
The seed word. The name.

With head preserve it.
With heart cherish it.
With inner speech say it.
The seed word. The name.

Patient persist in it
Each time replacing it
For your Lord's sake say it
Gently letting it fall,
The seed word. The name.

With head preserve it.
With heart cherish it.
With inner speech say it.
The seed word. The name.

GETHSEMANE PRAYER

*There, where eternity brushed Savile Row,
Stirring the surface world
I found Gethsemane.*

*Seeing some sad in soul
Sorrow sprang suddenly
Opened the hidden heart
Onto Gethsemane.*

*Lifting too far the cup,
There lost my secret self,
Finding its better part
There, in Gethsemane.*

*Green is the great world vine
Adam made adamant,
Ancient its layered leaves
Shading Gethsemane.*

*Pressing from memory
Wines of reunion
Springing to permanence
There, in Gethsemane.*

*Sudden a dark door closed.
Time's Masque began again:
Quick did the silver run
After Gethsemane.*

*If you can understand
This dedication,
Remember your bough-brothers,
Still, so still,
Here in Gethsemane.*

London, 1969

LENT IS A TIME TO SING

Lent, and the bud breaks bounds of winter stillness,
Green flood rushing, bright life washing
Away the gray days of winter, the damp, the decay.
Early and long the insistent birds sing
Hymns to the death of darkness,
Psalms to Spring's heady incense.
And we, fat in the ways of winter,
Thick of coat and chairbound.
We see Lent as a sleep, a denial of life.
Yet 'tis we are blind,
Set in the cold ways of winter,
Fearing the warmth
That would thaw.
For birth of man
A child goes down to death.
For summer's joys
The dark of days
Must melt before the sun.
Come, let us joy in simple ways,
And Spring...
Lent is a time to sing.

London, 1969

RECOLLECTION

I

*Without the Indwelling
There could be no outgoing.
Without the outgoing
There could be no fall.
Without the fall,
There could be no raising.
Without the raising,
There could be no growth.
Without growth,
There could be no
Giving and taking in marriage.
Without union,
There could be nothing begotten.*

*Without begetting,
There would be no sons of heaven.
Without sons of heaven
Earth would be born into darkness.
Without light,
Nothing would know the Indwelling.
Without Knowledge,
All would be only illusion.
Being illusion,
All things, forgotten, would die.*

II

*In the rejoicing and in the seeking,
In all the riding, and in the walking,
In the awaking, and in the sleeping
I will remember,
I will remember,
I will remember.*

*In every meeting, and in avoiding,
Deep in the loving, sharp in the hating,
Strong in the moving, still in the waiting,
I will remember,
I will remember,
I will remember.*

*In the arousing and in the falling,
Loud in the shouting, patient in hearing,
Strong in the going, meek in the taking
I will remember,
I will remember,
I will remember.*

*In the enjoying and in the fearing,
Clear in the looking, dark in the dodging,
Tall in the singing, lonely in grieving
I will remember,
I will remember,
I will remember.*

DEDICATION

That which you have always
Yet never see.
Seek it!

The food that is always given
Yet never tasted.
Eat it!

The life that all live
Yet none know.
Live it!

The road that you walk already,
Yet still seek.
Follow it!

Drawn by that which is.
Fed by everlasting food.
Living the only life
You have been given.
These are the Way.

HYMN TO IACCHUS

Now who will dance?
He who may hear the flute
That speaks directly to the unleashed feet;
He who can hear the heartbeat of the stars
With patient ears,

Now we will dance, and dance,
And dance away the days,
To men, as fools,
To gods, brief flowers of praise.
Now we will dance, and dance,
And dance away the years:
Time danced away,
Away are fled all fears.

Now we will dance, and dance,
And dance the step of light,
For he who dances steps of joy
Shall joy throughout the night.

PARDES RIMMONIM

God knows, the sad glory of Gehinnom
Turns every prayer to ashes.
Even our jokes are no longer funny,
And the proud tower of our knowledge stands
Mute-accusing finger: a desert tumescence
Scratching the leaden sky for heaven.
Pardes Rimmonim! And from the relieving rain
The bindweed springs its cruel beauty,
Embalming the patient seed,
Spangling sand's brief garden in viridian,
trailing putty-fingered to the sea.

Seed among seed, and some to spring,
And some to bind, and some to die,
All first to war in their strange way
For sun and shower, for earth and ear,
And one alone among them all
Is you.

God knows, the germination of the eternal
Tests all impatience.
Even the grasses of goodwill
Wilt in the waiting.
But who shall hurry the timeless?

I dare not. Not I.
Impatience too shall die
Ere that old trunk breaks earth
To put on green
And smallest seed
As largest tree is seen.

Pardes Rimmonim? Is it still there, the Tree of Life?
Under the bindweed, under the bindweed bound
Its richest beauty is its wound,
Its life lies secret underground,
Its leaves sport still with death.

Seed among seed, and some to spring,
And some to bind, and some to die.
Yet first to speak, in their old way,
Of sun and shower, of earth and air.
The one that first stood, standing last,
Is you.

London, 1970

THE LOVE OF WOMAN

Sharp need of nature strides the lowest rung
Of love's long ladder, its song early sung
To tell the lover love is reaching through
The world of works, yet always telling true.

    Here lies my weakness,
    Here my greatest sin;
    My heart's in nothing
    That you are not in.

The power of passion stands the middle ground
As moon to soul-sun's glory, echo to the sound
Of His great grace, the Spirit's power
That now may plough the ground to wait the sower.

    Here lies my weakness,
    Here my greatest sin;
    My heart's in nothing
    That you are not in.

To love of woman at its utmost peak
The many tongues of silence softly speak,
To tell the lover that, when freed of pride
Naught shall this love from love of God divide.

    Here dies my weakness,
    Here decays my sin;
    My heart's in nothing
    That Thou art not in.

V

SOME SHORT POEMS

TWO-EDGED SWORD

Love is a two-edged sword. No space divides
The heart that silent stands
From the high peak of Eros' busy flight:
Each rises level in the night.
Only the years, or sorrow's sword will tell
Which love's of Heaven,
which of hell.

WORK

To hear a pin drop when the thunder rolls.
To see eternity within a spark.
To sense the qualities within men's souls
As they who read life's meaning in the dark,
To walk with sages and to suffer fools
Is all man's work.

MAY SONG

O summer song,
O summer song,
The turn of spring
Is yearning me
Toward that deep
And flaming stream
Slow burning to the sea.
So long, so long
This river runs
Its way from you
To me.

O summer song,
O summer song,
The flush of may
Is stealing me
Towards the rhododendron day
That binds
The splintered sinews now
Into the newborn hay
So far, so far
The pulse of Spring
Can bind two hearts
To joy.

BUT ONE SOLUTION

So close two may be joined, it seems
That fear and pain
Raised in the one, may pierce two hearts alike
So as to divide the one flesh,
So as to embattle bruised minds,
That there's no resolution in the ways
Laid down by precedent.

How then may we find peace, who are so joined
That pain feeds pain in perfect union?

Where lies this union of hearts but in the rock
Of our unchanging substance, that our fate
So twined together, so conjoined
That each departure from our true estate
Breaks through an undefended gate
Upon the other.

How then find we our peace, so joined in truth
That each evasion tears the soul's fair flesh
Discounting distance?

*To those called to this high and painful grace
But one solution stands the test of time;
And that the high solution of the quest
To be oneself, to leave alone all else
Flee all pretension, cast aside the past
And come to joy in silence at the last.*

Bristol, 1965

EMBER SINGS
TO THE TALL TREES

O still. Be still.
Leave the incessant whirl
And rest on me a moment
And be still.

Sun, moon and sap shaped these
High foliated trees
Then wind's soft shaping
Wove the leaves
Each leaf leaping in waves of praise.
O still. Be still.
Leave the incessant whirl
And rest on me a moment
And be still.

Tide, fire and forced birth
First washed the spark-Earth
Then wave woke
Deep in dark heartsease
Wrote the round rhythms of praising seas.
O still. Be still.
Leave the incessant whirl
And rest on me a moment
And be still.

London, 1969

O MOST KIND COMFORT

Into the mirror, into the mirror fall.
If soul shall answer, is it soul shall call?
Into the river. Into the river deep,
Cast secret stirring - soul sink back to sleep:
For life's too long to keep a watching brief
When comfort steals, soft as any thief,
Upon the body, and through body steals the mind
O most kind comfort, nothing's more unkind,
No joy remains when comfort steals away,
Leaves soul in sleep to wait another day.

London, 1970

HELEN OF THE THOUSAND FACES

Always, you were around, burning into my eyes
When the stormclouds passed:
You smiled off the wet rocks
of the bleak Northumbrian coast
Before I had words to ratify your existence:
Off a sunrise sea down Devon,
Smiled through the high mists,
Under the cedar trees, in the still vaulting
Of the great cathedral.
Even in a railway station
Under a lowering Midland sky, smiled.
But I, blind, said
'I have not met my beloved'.
And blind, walked on.
A poet, purblind to all but words.
You, beauty, dumb to speak your singing truth
In a world that has lost its ears.

London, 1971

THE WELLS OF WISDOM

Be damned to self-doubt:
We met once in the deep dark
Of that other space
Sparked my sad cells to so bright life
Sung with sharp song of certain love
That etched all future thought
With that sweet sense
Of your continued absence
As we did part. Since then you lay
In the fast-fleeting corner of an eye
'Til I outgrew the hot blood of my youth
And tired of questioning the tattered clouds,
Of parsing trees with logic, to return
Hot on the hidden motives of the dream
Shaped by the sore-pressed sadness of the blood.
Now I am bold to seek your hidden star
In all the wells of wisdom.

Now no more dreams.
That one last walk with nightspawn; troubled bed
And the black-oiled rivers of the past
That lead me back to darkness. Mother Earth
Agape with night and silence leads me in
Under the roiling currents of her spring
To drink the draught of nightshade and forget
Sleep's other world of wishes and of fears,

My inward ancestors interred in unblest ground,
My foiled intentions and my dreams of power.
After a troubled summer dies the flower
Blighted by dreams of incest with the past —
And winter waits
For that new growth that springs from fire-black ground
To take anew the shape within the seed
And bear it pure upon the newborn land.

Now must I take the waiting part,
So Helen, wait
Witch o'the winter, dear heart of the dream,
Thy Circe-self shall no more bind the swine,
Thy beauty rule no more, nor thy glad warmth
Distract the watcher from your troubled eye
Where gape the black pits of your sleeping soul.
Love's not complete
Whose sacrament is servitude, and whose slow hope
Is simply for an end to some dull ache.
It lacks true strength,
'Til wisdom's firm to wake its primal voice
However death may drum.

Finished Newbury, Massachusetts, 1991

ICARUS

You have known me weeping.
You have known me sleeping.
You have known me fallen
To the sad and landlocked sea.
You have never seen me
As I used to be.
One answer can I give you,
If you ask me why:
'Icarus fell
Because he flew too high.'

You have known my mask,
And the blindness of my task.
You have known me empty
In the days of my despair:
Never known me other
Than a lonely brother.
Now that I can answer,
Thus will my tale run:
'Icarus flew
In the heat of the sun.'

London, 1971

VI

BROTHER CAIN

A long early poem, part of which was published in Universities and Left Review, London, about 1960.

BROTHER CAIN

For Gee, for whom time stopped in the mud of the Western Front.

And Cain talked with Abel, his brother,
And it came to pass
That when they were in the field,
Cain rose up against Abel, his brother, and slew him.

I

Where were you, Brother Cain
When the warfare came again
And the dead returned by habit to their posts.

Hot shiny steel and the soft green glow
Of the screen slow-revolving painting the sea
In lights and darks upon the domed glass. Silence
Yet, lurking below, the heavy heart
The humming, hissing turbine, surge of steam.
Patience. Slow the fireflies crawl along the screen
Tracked on the dials, corrected the miles
Closing to yards, the roll forgotten as the guns
Follow the nimble fingers of the god
Who squats, humming to himself, in the gyroscope.

The peak crawls along the grassy line
As the minutes pass; swallows the yards
As the hungry fan hums through the silence.

'Range...' the snapping switch, 'Locked on!'
The bowed head, the strain of waiting
Second by second, when will the word...

'FIRE!'

The walls leap at the frightened face
With sudden thunder. The numb wires themselves
In shock cavort, the screen writes frightened words
In a strange language — machines afraid of death?

Then the still waiting and the jar
Of shell-shot spray seeping through the air-vent
In agony of shell torn air.

What is it for, what
Makes Cain of ordinary man, and arms him
With guns and fighting spirit?
Why am I here?
Like the unblinking hypnotic of the cobra
My eye stares static at the screen
Sees rushing hills upon the grassy line ...
Hurled messengers of death, how near they come
How near, growing upon the screen,
My beating heart
Is swollen up to burst and make an end.

Father, I am not ready, in this cruelty
Give me an hour more to make my peace,
Give me a minute, give me....
It is too late!

These bumbling hornets sing to me...
You'll come to me, my dear dear brother,
I need thee, as I need no other.
When will you change your ways,
My brother Cain?

II

I fought along the Somme upon that most historic day,
And I might have been in khaki,
Might have been in field gray,
But I thought that I was winning
'Til I heard an angel say
"So you're back on earth again, my Brother Cain."

Stand-to with the dawn, sloughed in the mud
Walled in by wounded earth, heavy of eye
Forever the waiting, yet it was yesterday
I was a dozen miles away, to rest and pray.

Somewhere far away
The lone gun stutters greeting the dawn
And howitzers crow thunder to the skies
Gouging the earth across the barren plain,
All death and putrefaction waiting there
Waiting for me. The searching sun
With hellish fingers gropes across the earth
Striking the glint of fear off bayonets
Massed like a forest calcified with time
In the two rivers waiting there across
The riven glades of that forsaken plain.

'Zero minus one,' a hand in anger raised or is it hate?
The stock held close, the bolt snicked home,
The machine takes over, the ruling mind
Is squeezed alone into a dark corner of my lonely skull
Waiting for hands to fall, and hell to come awake.

First pressure, a shifting target shadow-seeking fast
The hand falls, the kick and acid cordite's reek
The sky carved into a hundred flighty kingdoms
By buzzing wasps searching out mounds of flesh
For something to sting.

Searing light and pain and fire
And broken earth and lives, and lives
Compressed to an instant passing into night
And the voice both loved and hated
Calling me, calling my trapped mind in the dark....
'Abel, Abel my brother!'

III

I fought the cruel Aztecs with conquistadors from Spain
And grinned at British seamen
Through the Inquisition's pain
And I sailed with Sir Francis
Buccaneering on the main
Where the lowest deckhand cutpurse
Knew me well as Brother Cain.

Scrubbed white wood, and the linstock glowing,
The gentle breeze. Square sails pulling
Over canvassed, sails soaking, linstocks smoking
Powder-in-the-barrel rope-ring shot home
Tamped and runout, primed and laid.
The fleeing galleon wearing ship
to bring her guns to bear.

White smoke, the ricochet falls short
A cheer, gruff Long Tom brought to bear
Ricochet, under their bowsprit. The sound
Of martial drums, soldiers manning rails
Weighting the galleon, slowing their working sails.

'Stand to the braces,' scuff of bare feet
Spray from the snapping swinging sails,
Three ships heel as one,
Three broadsides from the lower decks.
If they only will
Hold their course parallel shot will fall short.
See, see, is she turning? Slow, slow
As her sides splinter. Into range her bow-guns
Splintering close-by those bulwarks,
Death smells close.

Eye along sights, twist of the handspike
'Maindeck, Fire on the uproll,'
Long linstock, hot iron
Hot powder, hot rope sponge charge wad shot
Ram runout fire on the uproll hot powder
Sponge charge wad shot
Ram runout fire on the uproll hot powder

Sponge charge wad shot
Ram runout fire on the uproll hot powder
Sponge, charge, hot, smoky, wad shot
Cheers! Ram, runout. Her mainmast! Fire on the uproll.
Into the sea! Sponge charge. Might be outshot?
Wad shot ram runout fireontheuproll hot powder blood
My blood, blood on the linstock
Misfire!
Blood in the powder reprime fireontheuproll
She's (if I'm not mistaken) sponge charge striking
Wad shot, her colours! Fireontheuproll
Cheers! Cease firing! Numb
Creeping numbness
Pale skin, blood, cold
Hard to breathe. Hear the voice.
So cold. 'Cain...'
That call again, echoing
Into the brittle halls of eternity.

IV

I drew a bow at Agincourt, at Crecy won the day _
I bore a sword at Blenheim, and a lance at Malplaquet,
But my memory goes further, to that prehistoric day
When last my brother called me 'Brother Cain.'

Hot serge and horses breath, the dust
Of hot French fields, dry corn trampled
An army grouping round a hill. Gleam
Of sun on armour, sounds of jingling mail

*A drum that strikes a rhythm, and the shouts
Of weary men, driving home stakes in the hard soil.
The feel of arrow straight and true
Straight and true from me to you, willow wand of woe
Death's dark dispenser, slender stick of sorrow
Replace it. A shout....
The Prince! Black armour shines like night.*

*Sudden a trumpet through the morning air
A line of men breaks from the many hued French.
Silence grows into sound of moving armour
Tread of heavy horses. A trumpet for England!
More horses. Two lines galloping to
Collision, the smell of blood, the sound of steel
On steel, horses rearing, panic squeal
Proud lances shattered, proud heads bowed to dust
Proud shields trampled, armour soon to rust,
The proudest Cains that ever were
Are doing what they must.*

*As the ball bounces, as the thundering wave
Drains silent back to the Ocean whence it sprang
The two lines part, like wrestlers drawing breath.
Slow as death itself the great French mass advances.
Kneel behind the stakes. Kneel and string your bow.
Flex the tautened string as only English muscles know —
Distant, the ratchet winch clicks on the stiff crossbow —
Let 'em come, the mongrel Latins,
We've a trick or two to show.*

*A sharp command
The thunk of strings
Notch, draw, release, some danse macabre
Is mocking peace, notch, draw, release
Now screams sound closer, loud as any dreams
The thump of the casual crossbow bolt,
And dashing, clashing armour. Notch draw release.
What is it for? Notch draw release.
Why do I fight? Notch draw release.
Who are these French? Notch draw release
What have they done? Notch draw release
To me... have they... notch draw release
Killed me, my wife, my lonely children...
Do I fear them, that they might?
And if they might, why - unless they fear
I'd do the same for them? Would I?
What am I here for? Notch draw release.
If I die who shall plough my strips
On the rolling Sussex down, who shall repair
The humble clumsy hut that I call home?
To live, have I to stop another man
Returning in his way to his wife and child?
Shall they watch alone through the dark night?*

*The bolt that cleaves my helm
Shall bear the name of Brother Cain
As the death of man for man
When the old fear rides again.*

V

I rode the plain at Philippi with Ate by my side
And I sacked most noble Carthage
With the cruel Roman tide
And I fought for Alexander
With a Captain's rank and pride
Till his horsemen learned to call me 'Brother Cain.'

The tramp of legions, choking pumice dust
Broiling heat and heavy packs and memories of lust,
Gasping incapacity to gain
More than the rest we must.

Numidian cohorts thunder past, dust on their armour
Night on their skins and in their eyes. On mules
And shaggy ponies unkempt Gauls, with slings
And spears, knives and greenwood poles
They passed.

Vultures watched from a washed-out sky.
I saw a dead man walking over sun-cracked sand.
A cloud passed over the sun, a shiver
Rippled down the marching ranks, strange chill
Yet see! Trebonius' helmet glowing red
And sunrise is half-hour gone.
Is it reflection of my death?
Which vulture waits to steal my eyes?
What dog shall watch my carrion bones
Lest mongrel breed shall share his prize?

The thump of drums
The pacing feet
Left right, left right
Thrust parry, thrust parry
White bleached pale face
Skull bleached death shroud
Left right, left right
Thrust parry, thrust parry
Thrust....

A lance of sound
The brazen trumpet calls.
Rattled cry to halt!

Four ranks deep across the plain
the legions stand and wait
Quiet breath and muttered oaths,
the white scraped javelins wait.
Wait, wait, a little cornbread broken
And a little water taken
And a little water sprinkled
On the burning burnished helmets
And a little water offered to the gods.

A shout
A distant trumpet - Anthony!
Taking the line as far ahead
Symphonic clash of cavalry rings out
Jingles soft prelude through the drifting sand
To Death's slow movement by his iron hand.

'The day of reckoning, fight well, friends.'
(What can we fight for if we're not his friends?)
Were we beguiled by honeyed words
'To fight for Caesar and be free'
Or do we fight alone for Anthony?
Or when he says to us that latter men
May speak again of us when Rome is gone
Is it our vanity hands us our arms?

The coiled trumpet brays its challenge loud
Two armies meet in sweat and sand and blood
Thrust parry, thrust parry
In out, thrust parry
Death not so soon for me, good ferryman
A while wait. ... no coin in my mouth sits.

VI

In death are all things joined,
All times made one,
All earthly dreams forsaken, penance borne
Mingling in paths eternal, each human form
Made much of, made much of in the pattern.

VII

OTHER EARLY POEMS

WHO CALLS?

*Who calls? The nodding willow or the ash
Jerking his head along the gale's flank?
Who sensed the storm born in the air, the flash
Of jealous lightning riving rank from rank
Among the stranded trees?*

Who calls?

*Who calls? Across the blown beach way beyond the tides,
Among the rafter-bones of herring croft,
Around the shell-shock stump parade,
A whisper through the cobwebbed sail-loft,
Through spindrift-twisted sand?*

Who calls?

London, 1956

BURROW BRIDGE

Turning of the dusty road
What hand of childhood plucked at my heart.
Said: 'Look and love, as you have loved ere now
These doors, these hedges, every perfect part
Of tree and hill and lazy running lane.

'With love you have been here before;
With love come here again.'

Stepping the old stone bridge,
What joy possessed my lazy stride
That open eyed I stopped, I saw, I knew
Another beauty here beside
That which the eye could gain.

With love I had been here before,
With love was here again.

Bristol 1963

JIRIAN

*Jirian, Jirian, we'll come together by and by
Where the tempest cannot move us,
In our palace in the sky;
But until the time has come,
Let us walk the studded way
That those gods have raised between us
Who are dead - and blown away.*

*For Olympus is defiled and Apollo laid to rest.
Cruel Mars, his sword is rusting
And the armour on his breast.
Now the power has gone from Delphi,
For no words can come from dust
And no help can come to mortal men
From the dead gods of the past.*

*Jirian, Jirian, we built an empire round the sun.
Well, the Goths left it a ruin,
So we'll build another one
But we'll build it where such random hands
Can never hope to reign
In the hearts and minds and dreams of men
It shall be born and then be born again.*

Their chariots are rotted now,
Their spears drifted to dust
Who fought to make their presence known,
In warfare put their trust.
But as for us, we've fought before.
We'll fight them if we must
But our words are a hundred times as strong
Writ in the bones and the blood of the past.

Jirian, Jirian, have we not held the crucial key
That binds the million minor gods
In the tower of history?
Watch, that we know when the time is come
To set those million free
To sow their seeds through the mists of space
At the ripening of the tree.

Jirian, Jirian, have we not known the sacred place?
Have we not met the Great White Fathers,
Known the master by his face?
Have we not served that changeless empire
Which shall never ever pass?
Then let us, hand in hand together
Turn the key, and find our peace.

London, 1972

THE GREAT EXPERIMENT

Who tries his hand at life to mar or make
Himself, his fortune and his merriment,
Though poverty his state, he has performed
The Great Experiment.

Who will he be, through folly to be wise?
Who wears the world's mask lightly, nor surprise
Unseats him when his images prove false
But, making light of it, diverts his course
Into the unsigned paths where beauty lies?

Who of misfortune makes a stepping stone
And, others hanging back, steps on alone.
Who travels with the caravan awhile
Yet knows that he alone can cross the style
To that lone purpose bred within the bone.

Who uses all the tools of alchemy
In their due time, yet after leaves them be.
Who, living in the world, will pay his due
Yet keep it to its place, where it be true,
He makes its power his own, himself makes free.

Who makes himself a place within which meet
The powers of all the world, yet jokes on it
So binds his heart to nothing and to love
With bands of iron, needs no more then to prove.

London 1969

HAD I SUCH HEART

Had such hands I'd touch you now
To wake the womanhood that sleeps
In your bruised heart. I'd twine with you
Such merry fingers as would make you leap
From stone to flame to happiness again;
Then lay you down in roses.

Had I such lips I'd kiss you now
To warm the womanhood that waits
Behind your eyes. I'd breathe in you
Such living zephyrs as would pitch your pipe
To great Pan's lay above a sleepy world
And light your limbs with laughter.

Had I such strength I'd fire your tired blood
With nature's healing and with gracious light
To bring you rest. I'd wait on you
Such sunlight hours of birdsong as would lift
A silver castle round your sleeping heart
All lit within the living.

Had I such heart my words would weave
A spell of beauty deep within your breast
To set you free. My eyes would drink
Your glory and return to you transformed
That crystal image bred within your bone;
Then joust with you for joying.

London 1971

WHEN YOU ARE THERE

*Like a bird from the nest
Driven out too young
My heart it stumbles and falls,
Yet when you are there
It slowly falls clear
And enters the place to which
All of life calls.*

*Like a child thrown in
To the deep end to swim
My heart struggles back to your shore,
Yet when you are You
It is suddenly true:
The ice-cap of ages
Beginning to thaw.*

*When the mind from its roots
Is removed by the storm
It will seek a safe place to alight.
When that branch too is shaking
With some strange awaking
The promise of day
Overshadows the night.*

Bristol, 1963

INCANTATION

Weave a spell of light around
The open mouth of the gaping wound,
From the flesh afire distill
Crystal drops of purest will,
Cast the bone and scribe the sigil
In the unrelenting vigil,
Sound the oft-repeated bell
Into depth of deepest Hell,
Cunningly, with ancient art,
Fuse the incense of the heart
Frankincense and will-fire blend,
Cold, cold, cold as hope
At wishings end,
Within the death-wracked husk strike fire
Turn heart's dark rivers now
To sun's blood bright
And, dawn now telling from the watching spire
Stride out, and drive back
Black, black night.

London 1968

THE FEAR OF FREEDOM

What is this life that we should cling to it
As, waking, we but haste again to dream?
From this dream, then, is waking so unwelcome
We bind ourselves to things both small and mean?
Fear we the Truth more than we fear the lie?
Who fears the light is doubly 'feared to die.

The wildfire wanes when bound upon the hearth
As weeds possess the cracks across the path.
So long the bindweed leaps upon the tree
That takes its bondage as its constancy.
This in one hand you know, by this you walk,
While other hand has understood the oak
Who shakes the thunder from her solar hair,
As far the kestrel falls upon the air.

Both the one freedom breathe, not taking thought,
The one by flight, the other taking root.
For freedom lies in sap, in pulsing blood
In the stout shaft that shall survive the flood
Of our small dreams.
Here freedom lies,
Where lies the heart,
Not written on the skies.

Bristol 1963

REMEMBER, MY LOVE

Remember, my love,
That the dance of the worlds
Is the loom that has bound us in one
That between the dark hour
And the unchanging power
Only the angels
May dare walk alone.

Remember, my love
That the dance of the heart
Mirrors the dance of the soul in its place,
Whilst the body in glory
May tell the same story
That those who love soul
May look on its face.

As by playing a role
We may echo the soul
And our actions foreshadow our prayers
Our passion on earth
May but shadow a birth
And the sorrowing heart
May leap up to the stars.

London, 1972

THE FOUNTAIN OF LIES

Close by the Wall of the World
lies the Fountain of Lies
Its cold crystal drops reflecting the deep purple skies
Each in its way; marking the path of the stars;
Commanding high prices, long sought in distant bazaars
The jewels of the dreamer,
The tools of the preacher and poet,
First fruits of the fall, philosopher's goal,
The warlock's high prize.
Close by the Wall of the World
This fountain must rise —
So seek on! Seek on for the Fountain of lies.

Bristol 1963

COULD IT BE YOU

What if the sons of man are many,
like wolf-boys lonely and wan?
What if they walk by the length of their longing,
What if they talk from the strength of their love,
What if they know, yet, knowing, are silent
Denied word or wisdom, each one alone?

   Listen my sister,
   Listen my child,
   Listen and turn
   From the voice of the wild.

What if the bringers of peace are awaking,
Ordinary faces, lost in the throng?
What if the tide of the times is returning,
And the sons of the day are sitting here learning?
What if they're building the hidden foundation,
Without expectation, each one alone?

   Listen my sister,
   Listen my dear,
   Listen afar
   For the song of the star.

What if the shepherd kings are awaking,
In farm and in factory right through the world?
What if the sun of the Spirit is shining,
Lighting the hopeful heart, kindling the true?
What if the men of truth, casting all fear aside
Made the decision to live what they knew?

What if the world was born new?

London 1970, finished Newbury,
Massachusetts, 1992

THE OTHER EDEN OF THE MIND

Seeking slowly, slowly find
That other Eden of the mind
Where no people play or talk
Where the lonely distant walk,
In the gaunt Gethsemane
Of the empty heart.

Weeping deeply, slowly sorrow
For the dying of the morrow
Where ambition falls apart,
And dreams but serve to pierce the heart,
In the gaunt Gethsemane
Of the wasted life.

Waiting now the tread and drum
As death's legionaries come,
Soon to bind and lead away
In the gaunt Gethsemane
Of the death of pride.

Now deserted, bound and mocked,
Mortal flesh entirely shocked.
Sorrow like a cloud o'erlays
All the pathways of the place,
In the gaunt Gethsemane
Of the inner night.

*In the final dark subjection
Stirs the breath of resurrection.
How shall we our thoughts deploy
When the sorrow turns to joy,
And great Eden's rivers flow
Making all the world anew?*

THE PHOENIX FLIES

Bright the once-pale Phoenix flames,
Bright as the song of the thousand-names,
Strong as the dragon, swift as the flèche
From Artemis great longbow sped,
Loud as the warring of the winds
The Phoenix flies again, my friends.
The Phoenix flies, see
The Phoenix flies
Her night-wide darkness through our skies.

As the ashes cool in the wide-wings' wind,
Dust-devils whirl in the desert sand,
Deep as a diamond, jungle-strong
The Phoenix sings
Her triumphant song,

Soft as the whirring of the dove
The Phoenix flies again, my love.
The Phoenix flies, O
The Phoenix flies
Her bright light high in the midnight skies.

WHERE IS THE DOOR OF SUMMER?

While the tight turn of time
Transits the median
Of our first meeting
Comes the light sleep of waiting
Shaped upon Ea's silence, and ensouled
Soft with the vesture of tomorrows joy
Toward another summer. Now lift clear
From Leth's idle waters, memories
Made pure by passion's passage to the past
That in their deep translucence show
The door to summer firm beneath winter snow.

EVERY INSTANT HAS ITS MEANING

*Piece together our brief journeys,
Our approach and our retreat,
Every instant has its meaning,
Every image clear and bright.
Memory moves far more true
Than the things we think we do.*

*Read the inner sense in gesture,
Fix the fleeting of a smile,
Every instant has its meaning,
There is truth in every trial
As a stillness sharp and steady
Bides its time, 'til time is ready.*

THE WHITE HORSE RIDES

The rain-dust gathers as the blue light wanes
And a silence falls on the Wiltshire plains.
The ox-horns bellow,
The clan-calls sound,
As Swoop the swallow
Strafes the ground.

A murmuring of many feet.
The hushed child cries
In the Autumn sleet,
And the witchfire smokes,
And the witchsmoke spreads,
Over the ancient chalk-laid beds.

The sun breaks through
Like a sodium flare,
Yellow globe flushing
The night-couched hare —
And a silence falls
On the ancient plain,
As the old stone feet
Are at rest again.

Yet fear wet earth,
And flee the storm,
Where the witchsmoke spreads
From the hazel flame,
For the short dark men,
With their flints and bronze,
Live glowering on
In their Wiltshire sons,
And the rain dusk hides
What the sun dispels,
The clans still muster
On the chalk-laid hills.

They say the white horse rides at night,
When the mists are low and the roads are quiet.
Of the massed black shadows by the standing stone
That pass in the dawn as a dream unknown
We will say no more, for such dreams should rest
'Til the bright sun rises
In the West.

TO BIND BRIGHT FREEDOM

Cast the dark past
Like camouflage
Across the fields of spring
That blind your eye
Where beauty lies
While fear takes loud to wing.
Nor take the present
In your hands
Lest love again should sting
The open wound
Of broken bond
To bind bright freedom
With a ring.

DID THE GREEN STAR

*Did the green star of Venus shine
So bright upon your birth?
And did the Sun of beauty stand
So high above the Earth?
Did cold stone Saturn's distant flame
Invest your loins with life?
How then blows through your silken flesh
The secret wind of truth?*

*Do the great spheres upon their rounds
Shape for you every move?
Or are you from that other space
Fed by the one true light of love?*

*Did iron Mars with heavy hand
So chain your molten heart?
Did Mercury present you with
The winged heels of art?
Did the dead Moon with strong demand
Divide your life's long path?
How then blows through your every act
The secret wind of truth?*

*Will the great spheres in their approach
Divide you from above?
Or will you once again stand straight
Fed by the one true light of love?*